Positive Thinking

Positive Thinking

A 52-Week Journal of Profound Prompts, Inspiring Quotes, and Bold Affirmations

ROCKRIDGE PRESS

KATHERINE FLANNERY

To my husband, Mike, a positive genius.

Copyright © 2020 by Rockridge Press, Emeryville, California

No part of this publication may be reproduced, stored in a retrieval system or transmitted in any form or by any means, electronic, mechanical, photocopying, recording, scanning or otherwise, except as permitted under Sections 107 or 108 of the 1976 United States Copyright Act, without the prior written permission of the Publisher. Requests to the Publisher for permission should be addressed to the Permissions Department, Rockridge Press, 6005 Shellmound Street, Suite 175, Emeryville, CA 94608.

Limit of Liability/Disclaimer of Warranty: The Publisher and the author make no representations or warranties with respect to the accuracy or completeness of the contents of this work and specifically disclaim all warranties, including without limitation warranties of fitness for a particular purpose. No warranty may be created or extended by sales or promotional materials. The advice and strategies contained herein may not be suitable for every situation. This work is sold with the understanding that the Publisher is not engaged in rendering medical, legal, or other professional advice or services. If professional assistance is required, the services of a competent professional person should be sought. Neither the Publisher nor the author shall be liable for damages arising herefrom. The fact that an individual, organization, or website is referred to in this work as a citation and/or potential source of further information does not mean that the author or the Publisher endorses the information the individual, organization, or website may provide or recommendations they/it may make. Further, readers should be aware that Internet websites listed in this work may have changed or disappeared between when this work was written and when it is read.

For general information on our other products and services or to obtain technical support, please contact our Customer Care Department within the US at (866) 744-2665, or outside the US at (510) 253-0500.

Rockridge Press publishes its books in a variety of electronic and print formats. Some content that appears in print may not be available in electronic books, and vice versa.

TRADEMARKS: Rockridge Press and the Rockridge Press logo are trademarks or registered trademarks of Callisto Media Inc. and/or its affiliates, in the United States and other countries, and may not be used without written permission. All other trademarks are the property of their respective owners. Rockridge Press is not associated with any product or vendor mentioned in this book.

Interior and Cover Designer: Richard Tapp
Art Producer: Tom Hood
Editor: Meera Pal
Production Manager: Michael kay
Production Editor: Melissa Edeburn

Illustration © Creative Market/Karamfila, Cover.

ISBN: Print 978-1-64739-056-3
R0

This book belongs to:

_____

Introduction

Congratulations on choosing positivity! By making this choice, you have set yourself on a path to becoming a happier, more peaceful, and more loving person, which may help you live a longer, healthier life.

Make no mistake: Positivity is a choice. I have been researching and writing about gratitude, mindfulness, positivity, and people's abilties to quite literally change their minds for years. One big thing I've learned is that our brains are hardwired to find and focus on the negative. Being constantly on the lookout for danger and working out how to overcome hazards over and over again helped our ancient ancestors survive. So, having negative thoughts, fears, and anxieties doesn't mean there is something wrong with you. It means you're human.

I've also learned that just because we're predisposed to this kind of thinking doesn't mean we have to let it rule us. We have the power to control our thoughts and emotions, but we have to make the choice to do so. Recent research has shown that purposely focusing your thoughts on what you want them to be can actually rewire your brain, which is plastic and trainable. Our thoughts and actions create and excite our neural pathways. The more we think or do something, the more pathways get devoted to that thing, making those thoughts and actions easier and easier.

Changing your thoughts to embrace positive thinking is therefore absolutely possible. Like any skill—reading, cooking, playing an instrument—it takes repetition and practice. That practice doesn't have to be hard, though. You just have to make the choice to do it—to be positive—over and over again.

I've been choosing positivity continually for some time now, and I'm not perfect at it. (No one is.) I still get angry and frustrated; I still get sad and upset. But I don't let those thoughts rule me. Instead of feeling powerless to stop negativity, and dwelling on bad feelings, I counterbalance those thoughts with good ones. I take whatever is upsetting me and recast it in a positive light.

If I feel overwhelmed with work, I remind myself how grateful I am to be earning a living, and on top of that to earn it doing something I love. If I get frustrated because I made a mistake, I remind myself of three things I did right and then think about what lesson I learned from the mistake. I bring my mind to the positive again and again, and it has helped me meet the world with more energy, boosted my creativity level, and upped my overall happiness. I even sleep better!

This 52-week journal will guide you in choosing and practicing positivity. Each week gives you an inspirational quote or affirmation paired with a writing or creativity prompt that takes just a few minutes to complete. These exercises will help you identify the kinds of negative thoughts you routinely have and reshape, re-form, and recast them toward the positive. You will also find simple activities that will help you bring your positivity practice off the page and into the real world.

As you go through the journal, you will train your mind to switch tracks to positive thoughts when negative ones come up. After you switch tracks enough times, you'll find your thoughts starting from a positive place instead of you having to actively bring them there. And when you do go dark, you'll find the light again much more easily.

I hope you enjoy this positivity practice and make it your own—take what serves you, leave what doesn't, and have fun with it along the way. Remember that the goal should be increased positivity, not perfect positivity. The former is oh-so-possible, and the latter is a myth, so go easy on yourself. Be proud of your accomplishments, period. And just think, in a year's time, you'll have made up your own mind!

Week 1

What you think determines what you become. Change your thoughts and you will change your world.

—NORMAN VINCENT PEALE

Take a couple of minutes to write down what you think about yourself. Then read what you wrote. Did you say anything negative? How can you reframe those thoughts to make a positive change in yourself or your attitude about yourself?

Week 2

I choose happiness.
I choose positivity.
I choose love.

Affirmations and mantras keep your mind on the desired positive track. Take a favorite affirmation or mantra and draw it below as a decorative sign. Meditate on its meaning as you draw.

Breathe in Positivity

This breathing exercise can help you feel centered and positive in just a few moments—including when you're upset. Close your eyes and smile, even if you don't feel like it. Then inhale slowly and deeply through your nose, focusing on a favorite affirmation. Exhale in a great gust through your mouth, imagining all your negative emotions rushing out with the air. Repeat five times.

Week 3

What I think is possible,
I can make possible.

Make a list of all the things you'd love to accomplish. For the really big items, write down the smaller steps you'll need to take to achieve them. Then get going!

Week 4

Be sure of one thing—yourself!

—ELBERT HUBBARD

Being positive means having a good attitude about yourself, embracing your strengths, and realizing all the things you're capable of! Create a symbol that captures the belief in and love you have for yourself. It can be a regal coat of arms, a smart logo, or even a pure shape—whatever you vibe with that you feel represents you.

Meditate on the Positive

Practicing meditation not only helps reduce stress and anxiety, it also brings peace and positivity to our naturally fretful, chaotic minds. Sit in a comfortable position and close your eyes. Slow your breathing. Focus on the darkness behind your eyelids, how peaceful it is there. For the next five minutes, reflect on something that makes you feel really positive. Meditate on that feeling of positivity, optimism, and joy. Focus on the sensations of the feelings. If other thoughts emerge, acknowledge them and let them go. Return your thoughts to the present. Remind yourself that this moment is enough.

Week 5

Every day is a new opportunity to be grateful, and enjoy the world, and improve it—in our own little ways.

—TERRI GUILLEMETS

List something you are grateful for today, something you enjoy today, and something you will improve on today. If you can, make this short list every day this week and see if your outlook changes, even just a little, by the end of the week.

Week 6

I have wonderful qualities.
I am capable.
I respect and love myself.

Meditate for a few minutes on your best qualities, your capabilities, and the respect and love you have for yourself. Sketch some objects, shapes, colors, or anything else that represents those qualities.

Start Something Positive

Pick something you've been meaning to do for yourself for some time—learning a new language, fixing up your bedroom, reading more books—and start doing it. Anytime you feel negative about your endeavor, remind yourself why you're doing it by listing at least three positive things that will come from your efforts.

Week 7

I am filled with love, and I receive love.

Write a list of all the people you love and who love you. Make it a point to tell them in the near future that you love them.

Week 8

I'm not afraid of storms, for I'm learning how to sail my ship.

—LOUISA MAY ALCOTT

Learning to navigate life with self-knowledge and a positive outlook gives you confidence and peace in calm weather and storms alike. Reflect on how you feel you're navigating your ship now—are the waters calm or stormy?—and draw your thoughts below.

Positive Focus

Remaining positive in difficult circumstances is hard, but that's also when positive thinking can help you the most. Think of a trying situation, and come up with at least three positive things about it. Then the next time you are dealing with the situation and you feel your anger or irritation level rising, remind yourself of the positives.

Week 9

The best way to predict your future is to create it.

—ALAN KAY

Realizing a dream begins with believing the dream is possible. What are some of your dreams for the future? What small steps can you take this week to start making your dreams a reality?

Week 10

I breathe in the positive.
I exhale the negative.

Take a few deep breaths as you repeat the affirmation on page 45. Then draw whatever comes to mind, be it imagery, shapes, or even just swirls of colors.

Positively Mindful

Mindfulness has been shown to reduce anxiety, improve cognition, and increase concentration. All it takes to be mindful is to be aware of the moment you're in—the sights, smells, sounds, and sensations, and your own feelings. Instead of sending your thoughts into the past or future, slow down and appreciate the now. Right now, look around you. Pay attention to the details. Are there sounds you don't normally register? How do you feel in this space? If your thoughts drift toward something you have to do or something that happened, think of something you feel really positive about right now.

Week 11

I control my happiness.
I decide my feelings.

Control over your happiness takes time and energy, but so does feeling bad. Make the decision to take control. Write down a few mantras that you can use over the next week to feel in control of your thoughts and feelings.

Week 12

The higher your structure is to be, the deeper must be its foundation.

—SAINT AUGUSTINE

What are foundational qualities that make you a strong, courageous person? Draw a brick wall foundation, and label each brick with one of your core strengths.

Visualize the Positive

Visualization exercises are powerful tools that can help you embrace confidence and believe in a bright future. Over time, visualization can help train your mind to naturally generate positive thoughts. Begin by closing your eyes. Breathe normally. Picture yourself in a year's time. You look strong, healthy, and happy. You are where you want to be—physically, professionally, romantically. Fill in as many details as you can. Imagine your emotions. Concentrate on this scene for a few minutes. Return to it several times a week, thoughtfully filling in the details each time, building its power.

Week 13

Once you replace negative thoughts with positive ones, you'll start having positive results.

—WILLIE NELSON

By conscientiously switching from negative to positive thoughts, over time you can change the tone of the thoughts that form spontaneously in your mind. What are some negative thoughts you routinely have? What positive thoughts can you replace or reframe them with? For the next week, try to recall these positive replacements whenever negative thoughts come to mind.

Week 14

I am unique in many amazing ways.

Your fingerprints are unique in this world—small symbols of your absolute individuality. Using a washable marker, color on the tips of your fingers, then press your fingerprints onto the page below. Write or draw on each fingerprint something that is uniquely wonderful about you.

Positively Grateful

Being grateful for what you have is in many ways the essence of positivity. It is the recognition of the joys and happiness you have in your life. Take a tour of your home, acknowledging each thing you have that you are grateful for, from the big stuff like a roof over your head to the little things like a memento from a trip that always makes you smile. Consciously associate gratitude with as many things as you can, and try to be mindful of that gratitude moving forward.

Week 15

Feeling positive is possible.
I can change my brain for
the better.

Science has proven time and again that our brains are changeable—the thoughts we dwell on and the actions we take fire up and expand different regions of our brains. Repeat to yourself that change is possible, and then imagine what your thoughts will be like once you have successfully shifted them to the positive. Take a few minutes to write down what those positive thoughts would look like.

Week 16

All of the lights of the world cannot be compared to a ray of the inner light of the self.

—ANONYMOUS

You have a fire burning within you that lights your path, your passion, your life. Draw that inner light. Draw your fire.

Practice Positivity

Training your mind in positive thinking is all about practice, and the more personal and meaningful that practice is, the more effective it will be. Look back through your journal entries, your sketches, and the activities in this book. Which ones resonated with you? Visualization? Meditation? Speaking affirmations out loud? Pick your favorites and practice one a day for a week. Use this week to begin a practice that you can develop into a regular routine.

Week 17

All that we are is the result of what we have thought: It is founded on our thoughts, it is made up of our thoughts. If a man speaks or acts with a pure thought, happiness follows him, like a shadow that never leaves him.

—BUDDHA

Your thoughts shape your vision of yourself, your perception of the world, and the decisions you make—in short, your thoughts create your reality. Some thoughts are hopes or desires that bring you to new experiences and happiness; others might be fears that prevent you from doing what you really want. What thoughts do you regularly have that guide your actions? Are there any you'd like to get rid of?

Week 18

I wake up each morning
with strength and self-love.

Tonight, keep this journal next to your bed. As soon as you wake up in the morning, say the affirmation on page 77 and draw, in a stream-of-consciousness manner, whatever flows from your mind into your hand.

A Positive End

Negative thoughts have a way of leading you down a track of self-criticism, upping your anxiety and jangling your nerves. A solid signifier can help derail these thoughts so you can regain control of where your mind goes. The next time you find yourself going down an upsetting line, say, "STOP!" out loud, and I mean loud. Visualize a stop sign as you do it. Then remind yourself of a favorite affirmation.

Week 19

I have great power.
I am capable of change.

What bad habits do you have that you want to change? For each one, write about the power you have to change it.

MY BAD HABIT:	I HAVE THE POWER TO CHANGE:

MY BAD HABIT:	I HAVE THE POWER TO CHANGE:

Week 20

My best friend is the man who can bring out of me my best, and your best friend is the one who tends to bring out the best in you.

—HARRIS WEINSTOCK

Surrounding yourself with people who make you feel like your best, truest self helps you stay positive. What comes to mind when you think of your closest friend or friends? Sketch objects or a scene that represents what friendship feels like to you.

Positively Not True

When we think negatively about ourselves, it's often in absolute terms: *I always say the wrong thing. I'll never find a job I love. Everyone thinks **I'll fail.*** This all-or-nothing thinking is absolutely untrue, and you can prove it to yourself. When you have a thought like this, come up with three examples that contradict these absolutes and you'll deflate this kind of thinking: *My friends often ask me for advice. I am actively looking for a new job. My family believes in me.*

Week 21

Nurture your mind with great thoughts. To believe in the heroic makes heroes.

—BENJAMIN DISRAELI

What are your greatest aspirations personally or professionally? What kind of heroics would they require? Choosing to do difficult things instead of taking the easy road? Making a leap of faith? Going against the norm? Come up with a few mantras that you can nurture in your daily thoughts to help bring you closer to your own ideas of heroism.

Week 22

Positivity begets positivity.

Write the word *positivity* in the middle of the page; then draw branches growing off it and write or draw all the things that grow out of positivity.

Positively Well-Rested

A good night's sleep is so important for your mind and body. It's the difference between being energized and enthusiastic about your day and dragging yourself around in a fog. This week, evaluate your sleep habits. Do you spend a lot of time in front of a screen right before you try to fall asleep? Is your bedroom dark and quiet, or do light and sound creep in, making for restless sleep? Is your bedding comfortable, or are you always struggling to find the right position? Are you getting enough hours of rest? Identify any bad habits you have and start changing them.

Week 23

I am filled with energy, joy, and love.

What energizes you and fills you with joy and love? How can you prioritize these things in your life?

Week 24

Nowhere can man find a quieter or more untroubled retreat than in his own soul.

—MARCUS AURELIUS

Meditation is a powerful tool for quieting the chaos of the mind, reducing feelings of anxiety and negativity, and allowing power and positivity to surface. You can meditate by simply sitting quietly and focusing on an activity, such as breathing or drawing, and allowing all unbidden thoughts to drift by without giving them your attention. For the next five minutes, meditate on the act of drawing below, allowing your hand to do what it will.

Positive Experiences

Doing good in the world is a surefire way to make yourself feel good. Making an effort to help others has the added benefit of boosting your sense of confidence and self-worth, and you'll meet other do-gooders, which serves as a nice reminder of how many good people are out there. This week, find a cause you are passionate about in your community—animal welfare, environmental cleanup, spending time with senior citizens, feeding the homeless—and volunteer to help.

Week 25

Everything has beauty, but not everyone sees it.

—CONFUCIUS

What are the most beautiful things in your world? If you're facing any challenges or hardships at the moment, what beauty or positivity can you find in them?

Week 26

My thoughts reflect my feelings, and I control both what I think and how I feel.

Reflect on the kinds of thoughts that go through your mind on any given day. How much time do you spend thinking positive thoughts? Negative ones? Planning what you need to do? Remembering the past? Make a pie chart below that illustrates your daily thoughts. Do you want to change the proportions?

Positively Forgive People

Harboring anger or resentment for people who have done you wrong only compounds the offense. Not only did something bad happen, but now you carry around an emotional wound that hurts whenever you think about the situation. Forgiveness is not always easy, but it does free you from that hurt, replacing negativity with the positive. Try to forgive someone this week. Push out the bad feelings and allow positivity and forgiveness to heal you. Once you feel you've truly moved past the hurt, reach out to that person with a letter or phone call telling them you've forgiven them.

Week 27

My life is filled with positivity, as are my thoughts.

What people, places, things, activities, etc. never fail to put a smile on your face?

Week 28

Your life is already a miracle of chance waiting for you to shape its destiny.

—TONI MORRISON

Meditate on what you'd like your destiny to look like and draw the shape of that future. It can be as abstract or as specific as you want.

Positive about the Past

Everyone has an embarrassing memory that haunts them. Though you can't change what happened, you can change how you think about it. Instead of focusing on the negative feelings of that memory, train your mind to associate something positive with it. Maybe you learned a valuable lesson. Maybe the people you felt embarrassed in front of still love and respect you. Maybe you're just happy to be well past whatever happened, living your best life now. Whenever this memory comes up, shift your thoughts to this positive aspect.

Week 29

If we want a joyous life, we must think joyous thoughts. Whatever we send out mentally or verbally will come back to us in like form.

—LOUISE HAY

List four or five things in your life that bring you joy. Throughout this week, try to bring your thoughts to those joys and share them with others.

Week 30

When darkness comes,
I can make it light again.

Dark and trying times are inevitable, but you have the power to overcome challenges and even turn them into your advantage by learning from them—by seeing the light in them. Using a pencil and starting at the bottom of the page, slowly shade from darkest dark to lightest light, imagining your attitude lightening as you move up the paper.

Positivity Playlist

Music has power. It can amplify feelings you're already having or move you to feel something entirely different. It can lift you up, energize you, and transform your mood. This week, create a playlist of songs that really resonate with you, make you feel great, touch your heart, or get your feet moving.

Week 31

I will use my many talents to make myself and my loved ones happy.

List your greatest talents. How have you used them to bring joy to yourself and others?

Week 32

You do not become good by trying to be good, but by finding the goodness that is already within you and allowing that goodness to emerge.

—ECKHART TOLLE

Sketch a self-portrait that reflects all the goodness that is within you. Don't focus on your skill level as an artist but on the feelings you want to express or inspire.

Workout Positives

When you get your heart rate up, a number of wonderful things happen. Extra oxygen gets to your brain, which promotes cell growth and plasticity. Exercise also increases serotonin, which boosts your mood. More and more, therapists are recommending their clients try working out a couple of times a week before seeking medication to treat anxiety and depression. This week, get in a good workout or two and see how the exercise makes you feel.

Week 33

To look at everything always as though you were seeing it either for the first or last time: Thus is your time on earth filled with glory.

—BETTY SMITH,
A TREE GROWS IN BROOKLYN

Take a look around you, literally or figuratively, and imagine seeing everything for the first time. Describe what your world is like.

Week 34

I am grateful for the little things.

Savoring your morning coffee, walking your dog, taking a hot shower—these everyday activities can increase your overall positivity and happiness if you remind yourself to be grateful for them each time you experience them. Sketch a few of your favorite things as you reflect on how good they make you feel and the gratitude you have for them.

Positively Loving

It's easy to let too much time go by without expressing your love and gratitude for the people you're around every day. But telling the friends, family, and even coworkers you see regularly how much you respect, appreciate, and adore them can strengthen the bonds in your relationships. Sharing positive feelings makes everyone feel good and keeps your mutual respect and love for one another top of mind. This week, make it a point to tell the people in your life how much you care about them.

Week 35

Today is going to be
a great day!

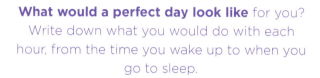

What would a perfect day look like for you? Write down what you would do with each hour, from the time you wake up to when you go to sleep.

Week 36

Clouds come floating into my life, from other days no longer to shed rain or usher storm, but to give color to my sunset sky.

—RABINDRANATH TAGORE

You have the power to recast negative memories as positive ones, so you can learn and grow from mistakes or bad times. Draw a sunset sky where the dark clouds of your past act to make the current scene richer and more beautiful.

Positive Entertainment

The media you consume have an impact on your mood and mentality. You're letting other people's ideas, emotions, and attitudes into your head, so as you work on fostering positive thinking, try out some positive media. There are plenty of shows, podcasts, books, and movies out there that have uplifting messages, tell stories of triumph, or at the very least feature adorable animals. Spend a week with just theses kind of media and see what effect they have on your thinking.

Week 37

I shall come, not as one who has escaped pain, but as one who has glorified it.

—MURIEL STRODE

Challenges often show us just how strong we are. It's easy to look back on difficulties and remember how hard they were, but it's important to also remember how hard you fought to come through to the other side and how resilient you were. When have you fought hard for something? Write about that strength. Are you unstoppable? Irrepressible? Resilient and brilliant?

Week 38

I am kind to myself in my thoughts and my words.

You can absolutely train yourself to think kind thoughts and speak positively about yourself; it just takes practice. In the center of the page, write "I love myself because," circle it, and then draw whatever shapes you like radiating from that center. On each offshoot, write a reason you love yourself.

Body Positivity

Feeling good and saying nice things to yourself about your body are essential in choosing positivity. Go look in the mirror, and instead of picking out your flaws, list all the great things about your body, from your head to your toes. Admire those arms that carry so much, those legs that take you so many places, those eyes that see so many things.

Week 39

I am a wonderful, beautiful person. I love myself.

It can feel awkward or vain to think about all your own best qualities, but doing just that is key to positivity and self-love. To make it a little easier to get into that mindset, try describing yourself from the perspective of your best friend or a close loved one.

Week 40

Life is not about waiting for the storms to pass. It's about learning how to dance in the rain.

—VIVIAN GREENE

Imagine yourself as a strong tree, as you too have stood up to storms only to be strengthened by them. Sketch yourself as that tree, with deep roots, a strong trunk, and branches reaching out into the world. Meditate on your strength as you draw.

Positively Natural

Getting out into nature, somewhere quiet and beautiful, can help you feel connected and peaceful. Take a walk in the woods, stroll along the beach, or hike to a waterfall—spend some time connecting with nature. Leave your phone off and try to be present for every step, appreciating the scenery and the delicate sounds that surround you.

Week 41

Life is 10 percent what happens to you and 90 percent how you respond to it.

–LOU HOLTZ

Disappointments and failures hurt, but they can change your life for the better, teaching you an important lesson or bringing you to an even better outcome than the one you originally hoped for. Think of some hardships you have faced. What are two or three important lessons you took away from those challenging experiences?

Week 42

I let go of negativity.
I embrace positivity.

Positive thinking is as much about letting negativity pass by without holding on to it as it is about embracing feelings of self-love and confidence. Practice holding on to positive thoughts by decorating this page with positive words. Focusing on them in this way will help ingrain them in your thoughts, making them part of your regular mental patterns. If negative words come up as you go, write them down; then erase them and write a positive word in their place.

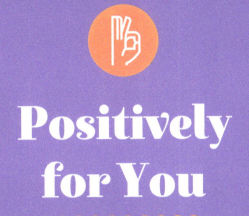

Positively for You

The world demands a lot of your time and energy, but taking care of yourself and your needs is essential to maintaining a positive mindset. We can't expect to stay positive if we feel overwhelmed and under-cared-for. This week, set aside a day just for you. Take yourself to the spa, on a hike, to a movie, to your favorite restaurant—do whatever it is you love to do.

Week 43

I create my future, and I am building something amazing.

What kind of life do you want to have built for yourself in a year's time? Three years' time? Five years' time?

Week 44

There is abundant reason to believe that optimism—big, little, and in-between—is useful to a person because positive expectations can be self-fulfilling.

—CHRISTOPHER PETERSON,
A PRIMER IN POSITIVE PSYCHOLOGY

Optimism is powerful. Expecting positive results goes a long way to bringing about power. Below, draw the feeling of positivity. What shapes and colors does it call to your mind?

Post Positive

Social media have a way of bringing out the best and worst in people. We tend to want to share the dramatic—our best days, our worst days, the things that overjoy us, the things that enrage us. These kinds of posts give us a skewed vision of the world that focuses on the extremes. For the next week, try to post only positive things and see how it feels and what kinds of responses you get. On the flip side, exposing yourself to other people's negativity can affect your view of reality. Is there anyone who routinely brings you down or makes you angry? Block or mute them for the week, and if you don't miss them, consider leaving them off your feed permanently.

Week 45

A good-natured man has the whole world to be happy out of.

—ALEXANDER POPE

A good outlook really does cast the whole world in a positive light. What things do you normally put a negative spin on that you could recast in a positive light?

I usually think negatively about:	I can reframe it by:

I usually think negatively about:	I can reframe it by:

Week 46

I have had many successes that I am proud of.

Reminding yourself of past successes improves not only your self-esteem but also the likelihood of future successes by reinforcing to yourself how capable you are. Below, draw a scene from one of your greatest successes.

Positive Speech

Making a conscious effort to get rid of negative speech is an important step in shaping positive thinking, but just as important is the addition of positive speech into your daily life. Try adding positivity to your conversations by pointing out when you like something, when someone did a good job, when you feel grateful for something, or when you appreciate the beauty of something. Saying these things out loud will reinforce a positive outlook.

Week 47

Anger does not serve me.
I let compassion and love
wash it away.

Think of a memory you revisit often that always makes you angry. Write about the memory, reframing it from a new perspective of positivity and compassion.

Week 48

When I let go of what I am,
I become what I might be.

—LAO TZU

It is easy to become attached to ideas about who you think you are and what you should be doing, but being able to change your ideas and yourself can open you up to new possibilities and paths to happiness. Draw a path to happiness and line it with the ideas, habits, and fears you might shed on your journey.

Accept Positivity

When someone pays you a compliment, it's easy to feel awkward and find a way to wave it off. If a coworker tells you what a good job you did, you might say that you had help, or if a friend likes a photo of you, you might reply that it was the best out of a dozen bad shots. Instead of dismissing compliments because you feel like you don't deserve them or you don't want to seem conceited, learn to accept them graciously. During the week, when someone pays you a compliment, take the person at their word, thank them genuinely, and internalize the positivity.

Week 49

As conscious beings, the only thing we need to find happiness in life is to perceive clearly who we are.

—KEN KEYES JR.

It is easy to focus on what you perceive as your flaws or shortcomings. Conversely, it can feel awkward to think about how wonderful you truly are, but it is that recognition of all that is good in you that can bring you to a place of positivity. Make a list of your very best qualities. Try to focus on them throughout the week.

Week 50

I am strong enough to do anything I put my mind to.

You can carry your burdens on your back, letting them weigh you down, or you can hold your responsibilities up high, confident in your strength to bear them well. Sketch yourself below holding the world high over your head. Focus your thoughts on the power you have to be strong, to be amazing, to do anything you put your mind to.

See the Positive

Routinely picturing the future you want is an effective tool for staying positive and motivated. Having actual pictures around you makes those efforts tangible. Find photos or illustrations online that capture the essence of the future you want to create, and use them as the background on your phone and the desktop and screensaver on your computer. You can even set up your computer to go through a slideshow of pictures and affirmations that resonate with you.

Week 51

The actions I take affect the way I feel. The way I feel affects the actions I take.

What are the main things you have to do this week? Write down how you'd like to think about each of them—energized, enthusiastic, challenged but invigorated—and practice bringing your mind to these thoughts as you carry out the tasks over the coming days.

My To-Do List	I'd Like to Feel

My To-Do List	I'd Like to Feel

Week 52

A world full of happiness is not beyond human power to create; the obstacles imposed by inanimate nature are not insuperable. The real obstacles lie in the heart of man, and the cure for these is a firm hope, informed and fortified by thought.

—BERTRAND RUSSELL

Reflect on what's in your heart. Acknowledge any obstacles to happiness that you harbor. Draw a heart below, and in it list the obstacles you face. Then color over them, concentrating on the positivity and power you have to overcome those obstacles.

Stay Positive

Positive thinking takes effort and commitment, but it is so worth it. It can make your life happier and more meaningful. It can help you appreciate the good and deal with the bad. It can make you a better person. Write a letter to yourself promising that you will do your best to stay positive, to love yourself, to embrace life and make the most of its twists and turns. Leave the letter somewhere you will see it often.

Resources

FURTHER READING

To learn more about positive thinking, you can check out:

The Power of Positive Thinking by Norman Vincent Peale

You Are a Badass: How to Stop Doubting Your Greatness and Start Living an Awesome Life by Jen Sincero

Handbook to Higher Consciousness by Ken Keyes Jr.

How to Stop Worrying and Start Living by Dale Carnegie

The Alchemist by Paulo Coelho

Mindset: The New Psychology of Success by Carol S. Dweck, PhD

FURTHER LISTENING

These positivity podcasts can help keep you on track and inspire you:

Happier with Gretchen Rubin

Daily Boost with Scott Smith

Magic Lessons with Elizabeth Gilbert

References

Armstrong, Brock. "How Exercise Affects Your Brain." *Scientific American.* December 26, 2018. www.scientificamerican.com/article/how-exercise-affects-your-brain/

Charvat, Mylea. "Why Exercise Is Good for Your Brain." *Psychology Today.* January 7, 2019. www.psychologytoday.com/us/blog/the-fifth-vital-sign/201901/why-exercise-is-good-your-brain

Cho, Jeena. "6 Scientifically Proven Benefits of Mindfulness and Meditation." *Forbes.* July 14, 2016. www.forbes.com/sites/jeenacho/2016/07/14/10-scientifically-proven-benefits-of-mindfulness-and-meditation/#4131d47d63ce.

Johns Hopkins Health. "The Power of Positive Thinking." Accessed December 3, 2019. www.hopkinsmedicine.org/health/wellness-and-prevention/the-power-of-positive-thinking.

Reynolds, Susan. "Happy Brain, Happy Life." *Psychology Today.* August 2, 2011. www.psychologytoday.com/us/blog/prime-your-gray-cells/201108/happy-brain-happy-life.

Sifferlin, Alexandra. "The Simple Reason Exercise Enhances Your Brain." *Time.* April 26, 2017. www.time.com/4752846/exercise-brain-health.

Acknowledgments

I am grateful to the lovely people at Callisto Media for the opportunity to write this book. Meera Pal and Wes Chiu were a pleasure to work with, and I'm particularly thankful for Meera's enthusiasm and support.

References

Armstrong, Brock. "How Exercise Affects Your Brain." *Scientific American.* December 26, 2018. www.scientificamerican.com/article/how-exercise-affects-your-brain/

Charvat, Mylea. "Why Exercise Is Good for Your Brain." *Psychology Today.* January 7, 2019. www.psychologytoday.com/us/blog/the-fifth-vital-sign/201901/why-exercise-is-good-your-brain

Cho, Jeena. "6 Scientifically Proven Benefits of Mindfulness and Meditation." *Forbes.* July 14, 2016. www.forbes.com/sites/jeenacho/2016/07/14/10-scientifically-proven-benefits-of-mindfulness-and-meditation/#4131d47d63ce.

Johns Hopkins Health. "The Power of Positive Thinking." Accessed December 3, 2019. www.hopkinsmedicine.org/health/wellness-and-prevention/the-power-of-positive-thinking.

Reynolds, Susan. "Happy Brain, Happy Life." *Psychology Today.* August 2, 2011. www.psychologytoday.com/us/blog/prime-your-gray-cells/201108/happy-brain-happy-life.

Sifferlin, Alexandra. "The Simple Reason Exercise Enhances Your Brain." *Time.* April 26, 2017. www.time.com/4752846/exercise-brain-health.

Acknowledgments

I am grateful to the lovely people at Callisto Media for the opportunity to write this book. Meera Pal and Wes Chiu were a pleasure to work with, and I'm particularly thankful for Meera's enthusiasm and support.

About the Author

Katherine Flannery is a longtime nonfiction editor and writer. She has worked on countless subjects, from humor to health to history to happiness, and she is profoundly grateful for each and every opportunity she's had. She is also the cofounder and editorial director of Tandem Books, a publishing studio. She lives with her husband and dog in Atlantic Highlands, New Jersey.

CPSIA information can be obtained
at www.ICGtesting.com
Printed in the USA
BVHW060143170420
577715BV00004B/8